INFJ
Heart, Mind and Spirit

The Ultimate Guide To The INFJ Personality Type

Use Your Natural Talents and Personality Traits To Succeed
In Your Career, Relationships, and Purpose In Life.

Dan Johnston

Cover Design by Scientist X Designs

www.DreamsAroundTheWorld.com

CONTENTS

WHY YOU SHOULD READ THIS BOOK

You know those people for whom everything just seems so easy?

Their career or business is always getting better. Their relationships appear happy and fulfilling. They have a satisfying home life, work life, and, by damn, never seem to have a complaint in the world. **Let's call these people the "Thrivers."**

Then there are those for whom life feels like a constant upward swim. At work, they feel like they don't belong. Their relationships are either problematic or unsatisfying. To them, life has always been a struggle. Let's call them the Strugglers.

What's going on here? Are some of us just blessed with good fortune? Is everyone else just cursed with constant struggle?

Don't worry, there are no magical forces at work - just some psychology. It has been my experience that there is only one difference between the Strugglers and the Thrivers.

The Thrivers, by reflection, study, or just dumb luck, have built their lives around their natural personalities. Their work utilizes their strengths while their relationships complement their weaknesses.

A small percentage of the Thrivers came into their lives "naturally." The careers their parents or teachers recommended were the perfect fit for them, or they had a gut feeling that turned out to be right. They met their ideal partner who complemented them perfectly. I believe, however, that this group is the minority.

Most Thrivers have spent years "watching" themselves and reflecting about who they really are. For some, this is a natural process. For others, myself included, it is more of a deliberate process. We read, studied, questioned, and took every test we could find, all in the name of self-awareness. We've made it a priority to know and understand ourselves.

Whatever a Thriver learns about themselves, they use to make significant changes in their lives. They change careers, end relationships, and start new hobbies. They do all this so that one day their lives will be fulfilled and will have a natural flow. They do it all to create a life where they will thrive.

This book is for Thrivers: past, present, and future.

If you once had your flow but can't seem to find it again, read on.

If you're in your flow and want to keep and improve it, read on.

And, if you're one of the beautiful souls struggling but committed to finding your flow and to thrive, you're in the right place. Read on.

Today you may feel like a salmon swimming upstream, but this is a temporary state. One day soon, you will find yourself evolving. Perhaps into a dolphin, swimming among those with whom you belong, free to be yourself, to play and to enjoy life. Maybe you'd rather find your place as a whale - wise and powerful, roaming the oceans and setting your own path, respected and admired by all.

KNOWLEDGE BRINGS AWARENESS AND AWARENESS BRINGS SUCCESS

I'm an entrepreneur as well as a writer. As an entrepreneur, negotiation plays a big part in any success I might have. One of the secrets to being a good negotiator is always to be the one in the room with the most information.

The same holds true for decision making in our personal lives. When it comes to the big things in life, we can't make a good decision if we don't have all the relevant information.

I think most of us understand this on an external level. When we're shopping for a new car, we research our options. The prices, the engines, and the warranties. We find out as much as we can to help us make our decision.

Unfortunately, we often forget the most important factor in our decisions: Us.

A Ford Focus is a better economic decision and a more enjoyable drive than an SUV...but that doesn't matter if you're 7 feet tall or have 5 kids who need to be driven to hockey in the snow.

When it comes to life decisions, such as our work or relationships, who we are is the most important factor when it comes to making decisions.

It doesn't matter if all your friends say he is the perfect guy; it only matters if he's perfect for you. It doesn't matter if your family wants you to be a lawyer, a doctor, or an accountant.... What do you want to do?

IF YOU MAKE YOUR DECISION BASED ON WHAT THE OUTSIDE WORLD SAYS, YOU WON'T FIND THE LEVELS OF HAPPINESS OR FULFILLMENT YOU DESIRE.

In order to make the best decisions, you must first know yourself. That is the purpose of this book: to provide the most in-depth, most relevant information on your personality type, the INFJ, available anywhere.

By reading this book you will:

- Improve your self-awareness.
- Uncover your natural strengths.
- Understand your weaknesses.
- Discover new career opportunities.
- Learn how to have better relationships.
- Develop a greater understanding of your family, - partner, and friends.
- Have the knowledge to build your ideal life around your natural personality.
- Have more happiness, health, love, money, and all round life success while feeling more focused and fulfilled.

FREE READER-ONLY EXCLUSIVES: WORKBOOK AND BONUSES

When I wrote this book, I set out to create the most *useful* guide available. I know there will always be bigger or more detailed textbooks out there, but how many of them are actually helpful?

To help you get the most from this book, I have created a collection of free extras to support you along the way. To download these, simply visit the special section of my website, listed below.

You will be asked to enter your email address so I can send you the "Thriving Bonus Pack." You'll receive:

1. A 5-part mini-course (delivered via email). This includes advice on how to optimize your life, maximize your strengths, and thrive.
2. A compatibility chart showing how you are most likely to relate to the other 15 personality types. You'll discover which people are likely to become good friends (or better) and whom you should avoid at all cost.
3. A PDF workbook to ramp up the results you'll get from this book. It's formatted to be printed, so you can fill in your answers to the exercises in each chapter as you go.

To download the Thriving Bonus Pack, visit:

www.PersonalityTypesTraining.com/Thrive

INTRODUCTION TO THIS SERIES

The goal of this series is to provide a clear window into the strengths, weaknesses, opportunities, and challenges of each type.

You will discover new things about yourself and find new ways to tap into your strengths and create a life where you thrive. I want you to have every possible advantage in the areas of work, play, relationships, health, finance, and more.

This book is part of a series; each one focuses on one "type." You will find that I write directly to you, although I do not make an assumption as to your personality type or your traits. I will generally refer to the type, aka INFJ, instead of saying "you." Not every trait of a specific type applies to everyone of that type, and we never want to make any assumptions about who you are or about your limitations.

I would recommend beginning with your type to learn most about yourself, but don't stop there. Each book will be dedicated to one particular type, but it will also be very valuable for family, friends, bosses, and colleagues of that type.

Even before writing these books, I found myself doing extensive reading on the types of my brother, parents, friends, and even dates. In my business, I would research the types of my assistants, employees, and potential business partners. I found that learning about myself got me 60% of the way, and the other 40% came from learning about the other people in my life.

If you plan to read up on all the different types, I suggest looking at my "Collection" books, which include four books on four types as part of a collection, for a reduced price. This will be easier and a better price for you than buying each individual book.

You'll find a link to all the other books in this series at the end of this book.

DISCLAIMER

I know this book will serve you well in discovering your strengths and building your self-awareness. I have researched and written this book based on years of practical experience including running multiple businesses, talking to hundreds of people about their strengths and weaknesses, and applying this knowledge to my own life to discover my strengths and build a business around what I do best. With that said, I must emphasize that I am not a psychologist, psychiatrist, or counselor, or in any way qualified to offer medical advice. The information in this book is intended to improve your life but it does not replace professional advice in any way, nor is it legal, medical, or psychiatric advice. So, if you're in a bad place or may be suffering from a mental illness, please seek professional help!

INTRODUCTION TO MYERS-BRIGGS®

I first officially discovered personality psychology about five years ago. I say officially because I do have some vague memories of taking a career test in high school that was likely based on the Myers-Briggs® instrument, but who really pays attention to tests when you are 16?

The Myers-Briggs assessment is one of many options in the world of personality profiles and testing. It is arguably the most popular, and in my opinion it is the best place to start. I say this because the results provide insight into all aspects of our lives, whereas other tests are often focused on just career.

The Myers-Briggs instrument is based on the idea that people are quite different from one another. These differences go deeper than emotions, moods, or environment, and speak to how we're actually wired to behave.

And, as it turns out, most people end up being wired 1 of 16 ways, based on four groups of characteristics.

This doesn't mean we can't build certain traits or change our behavior. Rather, knowing your personality type is an opportunity to learn which traits come most naturally to you and which areas you may find challenging or need to invest time in developing.

Your type provides a platform to understand yourself and create a plan for personal growth based on your unique personality strengths and weaknesses.

It is also an opportunity to understand the people around you and get to the root of many conflicts. In fact, you may find that understanding the different types and how others relate to you is the most valuable aspect of the Myers-Briggs instrument.

THE 16 TYPES AND 4 GROUPS

In total there are 16 different personality types that are described by a unique series of four letters.

At first, the types appear confusing, but they are really quite simple.

Each type is based on one of two modes of being or thinking for each of the four letters.

E (extrovert) or I (introvert)

N (intuitive) or S (sensing)

T (thinking) or F (feeling)

P (perceiving) or J (judging)

Now, don't pay too much attention to the words tied to each letter because they don't actually offer a great description for the characteristic.

In just a second, I'll share my explanation for each letter. But just before this, I want to share an important point to remember: Personality analysis and profiling is a bit of an art, as well as a science. In other words, since people are so diverse, the descriptions and results aren't always black and white. Some people have a strong preference for one mode or the other, but others are closer to the middle. It's natural for all of us occasionally to feel or demonstrate traits of the other types.

What The Four Letters Mean

As you know, there are four letters that make up your personality type.

At first, these letters can be a little confusing, especially since their descriptions aren't the most telling. But by the end of this chapter, you'll feel like an expert and have no problem explaining what each of the letters means.

For the first letter in your type, you are either an E or an I.

The E or I describes how you relate with other people and social situations.

Extroverts are drawn to people, groups, and new social situations. They are generally comfortable at parties and in large groups.

Introverts are more reserved. This is not to say that Introverts do not enjoy people, they do. Introverts are just happier in smaller groups and with people they know and trust, such as friends or family. Keep in mind, this does not mean that Introverts are incapable of mastering social skills if they must. Rather, they just don't find the process as exciting or enjoyable as an Extrovert would.

"The Deal Breaker": For some people E or I is obvious. For others, the line is blurred. This question will make your choice clear: "Does being around new people or groups add to or drain your energy? If you spent an entire day alone would you feel "off" or bad, or would you be just fine?" If you can spend a day or two alone without feeling bad, or if spending a few hours in a group of people leaves you feeling tired, well then, congratulations, you are an Introvert.

While Extroverts may often steal a lot of the attention in a room, Introverts often have the upper hand. While many Extroverts crave the spotlight, Introverts are able to sit back and calmly observe, learning more about a situation and making their contributions more meaningful and impactful.

Further, Introverts have the ability to work alone for long periods. In many professions, such as writing, this is a significant advantage.

INFJs are Introverts. This is why INFJs are so capable at working alone, are self-sufficient, and are usually not interested in building large social groups.

For the second letter, you are either an N or an S.

This trait describes how you interact with the world.

Those with the intuitive trait (N) tend to be introspective and imaginative. They enjoy theoretical discussions and "big picture" kind of ideas. For an extreme example, imagine a philosophy professor with a stained suit jacket and a terribly messy office.

Of course, this isn't the reality for most N's. Most intuitive people live a happy and fulfilled life full of new ideas and inspirations and have little trouble managing the day-to-day aspects of their lives.

N's have an exceptional imagination and ability to form new ideas, tell stories, and inspire those around them.

Those with the sensor trait are observant and in touch with their immediate environment. They prefer practical, "hands on" information to theory. They prefer facts over ideas. For an extreme example, think of a mechanic or military strategist.

INFJs have the intuitive trait. This is why they're attracted to ideas and have a natural problem-solving ability.

Third, you are either a T or an F.

This trait describes how you make decisions and come to conclusions, as well as what role emotions play in your life.

Those with the thinker trait are "tough-minded." They tend to be objective and impersonal with others. This can make them appear uncaring, but they are generally very fair. Those with the thinking trait rely on logic and rational arguments for their decisions. The "T" trait would be common among (successful) investors and those who need to make impersonal and objective decisions in their careers.

Those with the feeler trait are personal, friendly, and sympathetic to others. Their decisions are influenced by their emotions or the "people" part of a situation. They are also more sensitive to, and influenced by their emotions. The "F" trait would be common among counselors and psychologists.

INFJs have the feeling trait. This makes them idealistic, optimistic, and sympathetic to other people.

Lastly, you are either a P or a J.

This trait describes how you organize information in our internal and external worlds. This translates into how you schedule your days, organize information, and evaluate options and ideas.

I've never liked the term "Perceiver." It is better to describe this type as "Probers" or "Explorers." These people look for options, opportunities, and alternatives. They tend to be creative and open-minded. They're also likely to have a really messy bedroom or office. Perceivers are happy to try a plan out before they have all the details because they know they can always make adjustments later on if they have to.

Judgers are structured and organized. They tend to be more consistent and scheduled. Spreadsheets may be their friends and their rooms will be clean... or at least organized. They prefer concrete plans and closure to openness and possibilities.

You would find more P's among artists and creative groups, whereas J's would dominate professions like accounting and engineering.

INFJs have the judging trait. This is one reason they are able to stay organized, focused, and disciplined while working towards a goal.

THE FOUR GROUPS

Since the original creation of the 16 personality types, psychologists have recognized four distinct groups, each containing four types. The four types within each group have distinct traits in common based on sharing two of the four traits.

The four types are:

- The Artisans (The SPs)
- The Guardians (The SJs)
- The Idealists (The NFs)
- The Rationals (The NTs)

As an INFJ, you are an Idealist.

Idealists are abstract and compassionate. Seeking meaning and significance, they are concerned with personal growth and finding their own unique identity. Their greatest strength is diplomacy. They excel at clarifying, individualizing, unifying, and inspiring.

The other three Idealist types are:

- The Champions: ENFPs

- The Leaders: ENFJs
- The Prince and Princesses: INFPs

To learn more about how all the types relate and interact, download the free compatibility chart at:

www.PersonalityTypesTraining.com/Thrive

INFJ'S FOUR FUNCTIONS

It is important for you to know what the INFJ's four functions are, even if you don't know the science behind them. For starters, all types have the same four functions: intuition, sensing, thinking, and feeling. The differences are in how the individual uses the function (introverted vs extroverted), and the order in which the functions serve as strengths.

This will all make more sense as you read this book and continue your studies.

If it helps to get you started, here is my best attempt to explain the four functions in human terms. Many online resources use confusing technical language and psych speak when explaining this. I'll try to do the opposite here.

Think of the four functions as your four potential superpowers. Like an RPG videogame, your starting character has certain potential abilities you can gain access to as you grow. If you select the Elf, you will have access to different powers than the Orc or the Knight.

The eight available functions are:

- Extroverted Intuition (Ne)
- Introverted Intuition (Ni)
- Extroverted Sensing (Se)
- Introverted Sensing (Si)
- Extroverted Feeling (Fe)
- Introverted Feeling (Fi)
- Extroverted Thinking (Te)
- Introverted Thinking (Ti)

Note that the E or I attached to each function is not an indicator of the individual's preference to introversion or extroversion. Rather, it is an indicator of how they use the particular function.

Which four functions a type has, and the order in which they are strengths, is determined by the types preferences on the Extroversion vs Introversion, and Perceiving vs Judging measures. I'm going to leave it there, as any explanation beyond this would give us both a psychology jargon headache.

In your early years, your personality is ruled by your dominant function. This shapes your early strengths as well as weaknesses. Over time, through challenge and experience, you develop your second (auxiliary) and third (tertiary) functions. You create a more powerful and balanced personality. You minimize weak spots, mature emotionally, and develop a diverse set of skills.

The key to overcoming most personality challenges is developing (strengthening) the weaker functions.

In general, we grow our primary (or dominant) function in our early years, our secondary function in our twenties and thirties, and our third function some time in our thirties and forties. However, this pattern assumes you're not being proactive or reading a book like this one. In your case, there is no reason you can't leap ahead a few decades and strengthen your other functions ahead of schedule. Actually, doing so is essential to your personal development.

How We Use Our Functions

In the following section, you will notice each function is described as either introverted or extroverted. This is an indicator of use.

For example, an INFJ has "introverted intuition." This means they use their intuition to internally process ideas and situations and come to conclusions. Their secondary function is "extroverted feeling." This means they interact with the outside world using their feeling function. It also means most inputs are filed through the INFJ's feeling function before reaching the intuition.

An ENFP has "extroverted intuition" as their dominant function. This means the ENFP interacts with and experiences the outside world using their intuition. For an ENFP, their secondary function is "introverted feeling." This means the ENFP processes their thoughts and judgments internally based on their feelings.

An INFJ has the following functions:

Dominant Function - Introverted Intuition (Ni): INFJs use their intuition to internally process situations and ideas. This is their most natural function and gives them many of their visionary and creative abilities.

Auxiliary Function - Extroverted Feeling (Fe): This in an INFJ's second strongest function and one they must actively develop in their 20s and 30s in order to create a well-rounded personality. Its primary use is to create positive connections and social interactions through empathy, understanding, and a desire to serve the needs of others.

Tertiary Function - Introverted Thinking (Ti): This is the INFJ's third function. While developing their auxiliary (Fe) function will help overcome common challenges, developing their tertiary function will help the INFJ reach new levels of success. A developed introverted thinking function allows an INFJ to notice minute distinctions, spot logical inconsistencies, examine all sides of an issue, and solve problems with minimal risk or effort.

Developing their thinking function may also help the INFJ be more comfortable with confrontational situations.

Inferior Function - Extroverted Sensing (Se): The Se function happens in the sensations and experience of the immediate, physical world. INFJs that develop this function may see benefits in all areas of life because of the mind-body connection. Some ways to develop this function include sports, spending time in nature, and building real physical objects such as models or furniture.

DISCOVERING THE PROTECTOR: WHO IS AN INFJ?

At this point, I'm going to assume you're an INFJ and are reading about yourself, or reading about someone you care about who is an INFJ.

I'm also going to assume you've read some of the basic descriptions online about INFJs and have bought this book because you want depth and details on how INFJs can thrive.

So with that, I won't bore you with a drawn out description of INFJs. I'll keep it short, and let you get on to the other chapters where we go deeper into specific areas like career and relationships.

At first look, INFJs can be mistaken for Extroverts and often have multiple personalities they share with the world. However, INFJs are reserved and very private individuals. They prefer to operate in the background versus the spotlight, and see little need to show off or stand out.

Despite their independent natures, INFJs have a deep caring for others and value one-on-one relationships. Within their relationships, INFJs strive to resolve differences, clear up problems, and generally behave cooperatively.

INFJs value personal growth and are conscious of themselves and their path to a better self. They look at ideas, events, and relationships with a focus on growth and the learning experiences hidden within.

The mind of an INFJ is a rich and vivid world. Spending much of their time in this inner world, INFJs can be complex, mysterious, and puzzling to those around them... and often even to themselves. They have a structured view of the world, but it is arranged in such a way that only they are capable of fully understanding it. This leads INFJs to be very abstract in how they communicate, mixing facts with hidden meanings and possibilities.

INFJs are usually kind to others and thus well liked. Other types will often consider an INFJ to be a close friend, however the INFJ is often hesitant to open up and fully express their feelings to all but their closest companions.

One reason INFJs are slow to open up and build close friendships is their sensitivity. They are easily hurt by the words or actions of others, especially those they trust. When INFJs are hurt, they may not express themselves. Instead they may withdraw from the situation or relationship that caused them pain. This can leave others confused and wondering what happened.

With a natural affinity for art, INFJs tend to be creative and easily inspired, yet they may also do well in the sciences, aided by their intuition.

ADVICE FROM INFJS FOR INFJS

After publishing the first edition of this book, I reached out to a group of INFJs. I asked them what advice they would share with a younger, perhaps less experienced INFJ that would help them live the best life possible.

I thought I would include them in this updated edition, and what better place than here.

You can learn a lot about a type by what they say, and also by how they say it. For this reason, I have made minimal edits to the advice shared here.

"Learn the difference between your thoughts and feelings. Embrace your anger yet moderate its expression. Always trust your intuition yet find supporting evidence. Gain qualifications to validate your vision and insights. Surround yourself with Rationals and Sensors. Although this may be challenging it will stimulate growth in areas that will balance and ground you."

"Do a vision board every six months, and take actions to realize it. Gravitate toward people who are supportive and think highly of you."

"Hire a coach to talk to who can help you metabolize feelings."

"Be True to Yourself First & Foremost. YOU are the best authority over the creation of your own reality. Discover your Life's purpose and pursue it with the utmost passion & persistence. Learn from your mistakes. True liberation must start within oneself. While you can't control anything outside of yourself, you have total control over everything within yourself. Live a Life of Balance of Body, Mind, & Spirit. True Compassion is Helping Others, Help Themselves. ^__^"

"Always trust your inner voice. Yes, take into consideration the external data being presented to you, but when in doubt, trust what your gut is telling you. Whenever my life has gone off the rails it has been when I have disregarded what my gut was telling me and followed the logic someone else convinced me I should. Don't do that."

"My 13-year-old daughter recently tested as an INFJ. When I think about what I want her to understand about herself regarding her personality, I would have to say I want her to know that she should embrace who she is and to be true to herself, not trying to change who she is because others think she should be a certain way. Also, I want her to know that there is power in what others may see as weakness. There's power in her quietness, there's power in her empathy, and there's power in her intellect. Lastly, that she's loved unconditionally."

"Learn to completely listen to what the other person is saying. Your intuition will 99% of the time tell you exactly what they mean or intend to say before they have finished the second sentence, but more often than not the other person really values somebody who has intently listened to ALL their words over somebody who dispenses advice before they have finished talking. So many people feel judged or dismissed when you cut them off without allowing them to finish, even if you genuinely "get" what they are saying. Listening to them intently until they have finished their story will give your advice/wisdom more credit.

"Also... when a person presents a view that is different from your own, I encourage you to try to completely understand why they hold this different view. I met a young INFJ (with a very strong J) who held a different view to my own. I could feel her putting up a mental barrier to what I was saying, she wouldn't even allow the possibility into her mind. After that conversation, I realized that I do the same thing (though less frequently now). It is a way of protecting your identity/beliefs.

"Learn to recognize when you 'block' another point of view, and then train yourself to figure out why the person has another point of view, and what their logic is behind that point of view. Realize that you can entertain a point of view in your mind without accepting it as your own.

"Instead of blocking, try to be investigating, ask questions, seek to understand."

"I will tell you something that I live by and if you like it, you can take it or you can leave it. This isn't something that I would say is exclusively for INFJs though.

"In my bedroom I have a corkboard. On it I have three notecards. One says 'Now,' another says 'Victory Is in the Moment,' and the third says 'Make a Decision.'

"Why do I have those things written and hanging on a corkboard?

"In life I have various goals. These goals have to do with my personal health, my passion as a songwriter, or even my role as a friend, boyfriend, brother, or son.

"In the past I have often thought of the goals that I wanted to reach and the sense of victory that would come upon reaching them, but victory isn't something that just happens. It is constructed. The victory that I desire is shaped with each decision I make now. When I choose to sit down and write and work on a song, it is a little victory building towards my larger goal. When I make dinner for my girlfriend and we talk about our days and I listen to her, it is a little victory building towards my goal of having a deeper and stronger relationship with her.

"So, I make decisions with my goals in mind and I act on them now and in these moments I am constructing my own personal victories as I reach for whatever goals I set.

"This is how I live. Again, you can take it or leave it. I just thought I would share."

"Age should not be the factor to determine how wise you are, experience should. This world is cruel, but it does not mean you have to follow its cruelty. Inner peace is the key to hold on to who you believe you are, without it you may feel lost. You will feel lonely to fight this lone-battle, and other INFJs may be emotionally supportive but this world is always yours to deal with alone. Every environmental factor will continue to prove to you that you are the odd ball, while you continue to look through a glass. Self-trust and believing in what you believing in is the hardest route to follow in this dog-eat-dog world. I am not an older/wiser INFJ, but I hope my feelings can bring some insight for you. Best of luck with the paper."

"Be kind to yourself, you will be your own worst critic so learning to treat yourself as you would a good friend will reduce the stress in your life.

"Don't be in a rush to meet some preconceived milestone - you dance to a different beat, so you won't be in step with your peer group.

"Asking for help is not weak - it's a sign that you know your limits and want help before you break.

"Trust that intuition about the ones you love. Words don't mean squat - actions tell you whether that person can be trusted with your love and life."

"Don't be afraid to be different - it's in our differences we find ourselves. Be true to yourself."

"Listen to your intuition, learn from your mistakes and others' mistakes (be an observer), plan and know when to take action, have hobbies, obstacles will come but they will go away, have patience but never stop dreaming or hoping, learn to love yourself and stop being so harsh on yourself. Most of all just have fun, enjoy the ride, know that life is like the Matrix. What seems to be so real is always an illusion behind it all."

"It took me a long time to realize (real eyes) that it's impossible to reason with an unreasonable person."

"Hold on to positive thoughts! We have a lot of emotional energy to sink somewhere, so why not the best place for them?"

"I'll speak personally. There was so much wisdom I took in (and still do) throughout my personal growth so I could heal, prosper, get what I want, but the most important piece I could only find within... and we can all access it in a blink of an eye:

"Gratitude, gratitude gratitude!!! Melody Beattie once said it unlocks the fullness of life, turning what we have into enough, and more. It turns denial into acceptance, chaos to order, confusion to clarity. It turns a meal into a feast, a house into a home, a stranger into a friend. Nourish your soul first! Everything else will follow."

"In your life, it's not about what happens, it's about what you make of it." This can be read in two levels:

1) That you are forced to see the world from the lens of your senses and

2) that you will decide if you like the world you perceive or not. In both interpretations the concept is the same though, that your experience of life can be changed by what is around you, but that ultimately being happy about it or not is up to you."

IN GOOD COMPANY: FAMOUS INFJS

As an INFJ, you are among some very good company. In this chapter you'll find a collection of famous and "successful" people who are either confirmed, or suspected, as being INFJs.

Do not use this chapter as a guide to what you must do or the path you must follow. Rather, use this chapter as a source of inspiration. It is a chance to see what's possible as an INFJ and what great things have been accomplished by those who share a similar makeup to you.

Personally, I have found great value in studying famous people from my own type, including reading their autobiographies. Most of us spend the early years of our lives feeling lost and trying to figure out our life's purpose or how we want to end up. I've found that studying those of my type who have found their purpose, and then achieved success, gives me a shortcut to understanding my own potential and the directions my life could go.

FAMOUS INFJS

Scientists, Writers, and Thought Leaders

Plato

Carl Gustav Jung

Niels Bohr

Mahatma Gandhi

Mary Wollstonecraft

Simone de Beauvoir

Ludwig Wittgenstein

Sam Harris

Dante Alighieri

Fyodor Dostoevsky

Aleksandr Solzhenitsyn

Baruch Spinoza

Arthur Schopenhauer

Noam Chomsky

Actors and Performers	Politicians and Leaders
Leonard Cohen	Thomas Jefferson
Marilyn Manson	Calvin Coolidge
George Harrison	Ron Paul
Daniel Day-Lewis	Woodrow Wilson
Al Pacino	Marcus Aurelius
Edward Norton	Robert Mugabe
Adrien Brody	Osama bin Laden
Michelle Pfeiffer	Adolf Hitler
Cate Blanchett	Ayatollah Khomeini
Carey Mulligan	Leon Trotsky
Derren Brown	Chiang Kai-shek
Rooney Mara	

INSIGHTS

If you haven't yet read up on any of the other types you may not notice the distinctions of the famous INFJs. Compared with other types, famous INFJs tend to be some of the best in their chosen fields. Whether it is Gandhi, Al Pacino, or even Osama Bin Laden, INFJs will commit and give everything they have to their goals.

GOING DEEPER EXERCISE

Of the famous INFJs on this list, which are most familiar to you?

_____

_____

_____

_____

_____

What are some common elements that you notice? These could be specific personality traits or characteristics. They could also include actions they have taken or tough decisions they have made. For example, going against the grain or choosing to follow a passion.

_____

_____

_____

_____

_____

YOUR SECRET WEAPONS

Aka Your Unique Strengths

In my own life I have found no greater success secret than discovering, *and applying* my strengths.

When we are young, we are told to be good at many things. For example, since schools are based on your average grade, most parents would prefer their child have a smooth report card of all B+s rather than one with two A+s and two C-s.

If a student is gifted in math but struggles in English, she may not be accepted to any university because her average grade would be too low. The whole education system teaches one to be "well rounded."

Yet, the real world doesn't reward the well-rounded individual, at least not exceptionally well. Those who receive the greatest rewards are those who focus on their strengths and ignore all else. Think of people like Arnold Schwarzenegger, Steve Jobs, and Oprah Winfrey.

Does anyone *really* care if Oprah is bad at math, if Arnold has trouble managing his personal life, or if Steve Jobs was a bit of an ass to employees from time to time?

Nope. No one cares because each of these Greats focused on their strengths and in the process created extraordinary lives for themselves.

Oprah (an ENFJ) harnessed her empathy and ability to build trust and bond with people to create incredible interviews and connect with her audience.

Arnold (an INTJ) used his focus, discipline, and strategic thinking to achieve incredible goals in fitness, Hollywood, and politics, despite being the underdog in almost everything he ever did.

Steve Jobs (an ISTP) kept his energy focused on his creative and visual strengths. His visions were so clear, and his innovations so impressive, that his social graces didn't matter.

Now, as you read on you will discover the unique strengths closely linked to INFJs. While you read this, remember that these are only the strengths that come naturally to you: You still need to develop and fine-tune them if you want to thrive.

AN INFJ'S SECRET WEAPONS

- INFJs have incredible insight into people and situations. Of all the types, INFJs are most likely to report extreme "psychic" like experiences.
- INFJs are both creative and artistic.
- INFJs are interested in systems and determining the best ways to get things done. Couple this with their strong drive to succeed, and you can understand why INFJs excel at achieving their goals.
- INFJs are natural nurturers. They make great parents, spouses, and mentors, because they can be patient with, devoted to, and protective of those they care about.
- INFJs will generally form very close and loving relationships with those they care about, while at the same time push the people in their life to succeed. This happens because of INFJs' very high standards and expectations of themselves and of others.
- INFJs commit to finishing what they start. If they take on a project or goal they will focus and work on it until they reach their desired outcome. They aren't afraid of hard

work. Their work ethic and persistence is genuinely inspiring to others.

- Overall, INFJs are bright and intelligent.
- INFJs' quickness stems from their perceptiveness and intelligence. As part of these same abilities, they're able to see connections between people, situations, and ideas that most others miss. This often leads them to create new ideas.
- INFJs can be great listeners and make those around them feel heard. This allows them to understand others and build rapport very quickly.
- INFJs' intelligence, combined with their focus, gives them the ability to grasp difficult ideas and work on one thing until completion.
- Like other NFs, INFJs are idealistic. They also tend to be perfectionists... and have the focus to follow through on this idealism. This means they always strive for the best and are often able to deliver it.

Highly developed INFJs will enjoy even more superpowers:

- A rare and valuable ability to step into a situation, quickly and accurately make an assessment, and then create an action plan. The speed in which they can do this, combined with their ability to handle both sides (accessing and taking action), is what makes this ability so rare.
- An impressive ability to understand very difficult concepts beyond what their "natural intelligence" would otherwise be able to understand. In other words, an INFJ with an IQ of 115 may be able to understand complex concepts another type with an IQ of 130 may not be able to grasp.

These two superpowers often give the INFJ an ability to appear "wise beyond their years."

In summary, a developed INFJ can be:

- Goal Oriented
- Very Driven and Determined
- Persistent
- Insightful
- Creative
- Intelligent
- Logical
- Focused
- Quick
- Caring
- Intuitive
- Supportive
- Inspiring
- A Great Teacher or Mentor

Keys to Using Your Strengths as an INFJ

It is important to find a career and relationship that allows you to use your strengths. Beyond this, it is also important to keep yourself in a positive mental state so that you're able to fully tap into your strengths and reach your potential. You will be in the best state to make use of your strengths if you:

1. Focus on goals that will bring a balanced happiness to your life.
2. Avoid situations rife with conflict or confrontation.
3. Realize you are unique among most groups and learn to accept other people (and their weaknesses).

In this and future chapters, you will discover "Going Deeper" exercises. These are designed to help you better understand and apply the chapter's content. If you're like me, you may want to write your answers down. When you bought this book you also got access to a companion workbook that you can print and then fill in with your answers as you go. You can download the workbook for free at:

www.PersonalityTypesTraining.com/Thrive

GOING DEEPER EXERCISE

Of the strengths listed in this chapter, which stand out as strengths you recognize in yourself?

_____

_____

_____

_____

_____

What are 3 strengths listed above that you know you have but are not actively using in your life, at least not as much as you know you could be?

_____

_____

_____

_____

_____

How could you apply these strengths more frequently?

_____

_____

_____

_____

YOUR KRYPTONITE

Aka Your Potential Problem Areas

You didn't think I was going to stop at your strengths, did you? As much as I say *focus on your strengths,* it is still important to be aware of your weaknesses, even if it is just so that you can ignore them more easily.

Below you will find a list of weaknesses, or challenges, common among INFJs. As with strengths, this is not a definitive list and do not take it as a prescription for how INFJs have to be.

Sometimes I will see posts in a Facebook group for a specific type where people seem overly proud of their type challenges. I remember one post on an ENFP group making light of how the poster had been unable to tidy their room in four days. While it was good for a "we've all been there" chuckle, I did find myself turned off by thinking about what a chaotic life this person must have.

This person chose not to fix their weakness. For example, they could have chosen to develop their self-discipline and, over time, it would become easier to stay tidy. They were also unwilling to just accept this weakness and find another solution. If they decided to embrace it, then they could have just hired a maid. Instead, they have chosen to suffer what they described as four days of agony simply trying to clean a room.

Common Kryptonite for the INFJ

INFJs' challenges revolve around their tendency to form quick judgments around their values and the values of others. A secondary challenge, tied to the first, is their tendency to base their own value on the perceptions or beliefs of others.

If some of these weaknesses don't really resonate with you, that's **good**. Do not assume you should be weak in an area simply because you read it here. It is very possible that you are wired a little differently, or that you've already developed beyond some of your inborn weak spots.

On the other hand, if you find yourself nodding in agreement while reading, take it as an opportunity to either improve that area of yourself, or accept it and find a another way to deal with it.

Note: You'll find more on "outsourcing" your weaknesses in the later chapter "Practical Problems to Common Challenges."

INFJs may experience the following challenges at one time or another:

- INFJs may be very sensitive to criticism. Often this even includes criticism shared with the best intentions (as in this chapter).
- INFJs may be very impatient with less intelligent people, people who think "slower," or people who disagree with their way of doing things.
- Conflict and stress can push the INFJ to angry states, and ongoing stress often leads to health issues, as the INFJ isn't great at dealing with negative states.
- INFJs may become pig-headed and ignore other people's opinions. This happens for two reasons: The first is their mode of operating and interacting with the world. This

stems from how INFJs are "wired" to think and process information. The second reason is their real world experience interacting with people. INFJs look back on all the time wasted arguing with people who turned out to be wrong. Because INFJs are very intelligent, they tend to have winning track records when it comes to the "right way to do things."

INFJs must be careful though. While they may be right the majority of the time, they may miss valuable insights and feedback by dismissing what others have to say too early.

- INFJs are rarely at peace or 100% happy with themselves or their situation. This positively contributes to their drive, but strips them of enjoying the benefits of their hard work as much as they should.

- Sometimes they have little regard for how others see them or in what regard they are held. This can lead to harsh treatment and offensive behavior or statements.

- INFJs may obsess over details that have no real significance to the big picture. This can lead to a lot of wasted time and resources. For INFJs, it's important to remember the 80/20 rule.

- If overrun by their weak spots, INFJs can become high strung and lose the ability to relax. This may lead to high blood pressure and health issues despite an otherwise healthy lifestyle in terms of food and exercise.

- INFJs are perfectionists with very high standards. This can lead to unrealistic and unfair expectations of themselves and of others. Their personal expectations fuel their drive and their self-criticism. INFJs should strive to maintain their drive while going a little easier on themselves.

A person of whom an INFJ holds high expectations will feel a great sense of motivation but they may also suffer from excessive pressure and stress, or develop resentment towards the INFJ. INFJs must be careful where they place their high expectations and use their exceptional perceptive abilities to know when to ease up.

- As mentioned earlier, INFJs may be severe in their judgment and treatment of others. This may play out in many different ways:
  - o This is especially true when an INFJ feels wronged. When this happens, they may struggle to forgive and hold on to grudges far too long.
  - o They may forget their sense of empathy and become intolerant and overly judgmental of weaknesses in other people. INFJs should remember that these people would part ways with their weaknesses if they could.
  - o They may get angry or impatient with people who don't "get it," or appear to be doing things wrong.
  - o They may be very pointed and cruel with their words without regard for the hurt they could cause.
- INFJs may become rigid in their value judgments of other people and external situations. This often happens without fully understanding a complex situation and thus is unfair to those being judged. When this happens, INFJs may get stuck in their ways and close off to new possibilities or approaches.
- INFJs generally shy away from confrontation. Life is good when the people around them are happy. This may lead to avoidance behavior, rising tensions, and unresolved issues lingering in their relationships. This situation worsens when an INFJ holds on to harsh judgments or grudges.

- As mentioned earlier, INFJs are very sensitive to negative criticism and yet may be quick to form long-lasting negative judgments of other people.

OVERCOMING YOUR WEAKNESSES

Many of the INFJ's weaknesses share a single root cause stemming from how their personality receives and processes information. You may remember that the INFJ's primary function is their introverted intuition (Ni), followed by their secondary function, extroverted feeling (Fe).

If they do not sufficiently develop their secondary function, extroverted feeling, the INFJ tends to judge things before really thinking about them. Instead of letting people, situations, or ideas enter and process by their introverted intuition, INFJ's problems come when they unleash their extroverted feeling first.

OK, sorry, that was a lot of psych speak. Let me translate. INFJs tend to judge things too fast based on how they first feel. This is worsened when an INFJ's primary function (Ni) is significantly stronger than their secondary function (Fe) and influences their feelings. Essentially, their intuition takes over the other functions and uses them to distort the outside world so it aligns with their internal viewpoint or identity. This causes the INFJ to pass premature judgment on people or situations, or to screen out information that runs contrary to what the INFJ believes.

To overcome their weaknesses, INFJs need to take a little more time to think about people, situations, and ideas before they decide how they feel about them.

Think about and process first, judge later.

Turning Theory into Practice

One way to develop this habit is to practice focusing on other people and points of view. Read autobiographies and stories. Take the time to understand why other people act the way they do. This includes understanding their value system as different but not inherently better or worse than your own.

During day-to-day interactions with others, INFJs will benefit from taking time to question their own judgments. Are you making an effort to understand the other person, their values, and their circumstances? Or are you jumping to conclusions and judging before running the situation through your intuition?

When new information appears that could threaten your value system, do you allow it to process or do you get defensive and dismiss it in order to protect your way of seeing the world?

GOING DEEPER EXERCISE

Of the weaknesses listed above, which 3 do you most recognize in yourself?

_____

_____

_____

_____

_____

_____

What are 3 weaknesses listed above that you know are having a significant negative impact on your success?

_____

_____

_____

_____

_____

_____

How could you reduce the impact these weaknesses have on your life, either by learning to overcome them or eliminating the activities that bring them to the surface?

_____

_____

_____

_____

_____

_____

IDEAL CAREER OPTIONS FOR AN INFJ

If you gave a Myers-Briggs® assessment to a group of a few hundred people from the same profession, you would see a very clear pattern.

An accountant in my martial arts class told me that of 600 chartered accountants who took the Myers-Briggs test at his firm, he was one of only three people who didn't score the same type.

This happens for two reasons:

1) Selection Bias: People with the personality type for accounting will tend to do well in related tasks and receive hints that that kind of work is right for them. They may especially enjoy numbers, spreadsheets, etc.

2) Survival Bias: Those with the personality type for accounting are most likely to pass the vigorous tests and internships required to become a chartered accountant.

We are actually much better at finding our path than we give ourselves credit for. In almost every profession, there is a significantly higher percentage of those "typed" to excel in it than random chance would allow.

Yet, many people still slip through the cracks, or spend decades searching for their perfect career before finding it.

This chapter will help you avoid the cracks and stop wasting your precious time. Below, you'll find a comprehensive list of careers INFJs tend to be drawn to and succeed in.

There are many INFJ career options included on websites and guides that I have intentionally excluded here. These include "good" career options in which an INFJ could easily succeed but would be unlikely to find real happiness or fulfillment. This list focuses on careers where an INFJ can focus on their strengths.

I have included only the options I believe INFJs have an upper hand in *and* those in which there is the highest likelihood to find fulfillment and success. There are always other options, but why swim upstream if you don't need to, right?

To be most successful, an INFJ should focus on work that:

- Allows them to support people in both a "big picture" context, and through one-on-one relationships and mentoring.
- Rewards contribution and revolves around a positive, conflict-free work environment.
- Encourages creative contribution and problem-solving.
- Allows the INFJ to explore new ideas and approaches, especially those that will positively impact others.
- Aligns with their personal beliefs and values. INFJs live by their values and must believe in the work they are doing.
- Provides a chance to see and experience the results of their vision and hard work.
- Occurs within a flexible company structure and work environment.
- Provides enough time and autonomy for the INFJ to process ideas at their own pace and follow hunches or inspirations.
- Acknowledges and rewards original thoughts and ideas with credit going to the INFJ for their contributions.

Further Thoughts

INFJs have an exceptional gift for focusing and achieving their goals. Don't set your sights too low and be cautious of companies or professions with a "low ceiling" for achievement or mediocre expectations for achievement. In many cases, you will outwork and outpace your colleagues and may become very frustrated if your efforts are only marginally awarded. Further, companies that set low expectations are more likely to attract average performers and the kind of "slow thinkers" that send an INFJ's blood pressure through the roof.

Set your sights on a challenging profession and you are more likely to find yourself surrounded by peers of a similar ambition and intelligence.

Some of the professions below would typically have this "low ceiling" but that doesn't mean you can't find a company that has raised the bar. Alternatively, consider the entrepreneurial route and starting your own company in one of the fields below, or placing yourself in a position where your rewards are tied to your performance.

POPULAR PROFESSIONS FOR INFJS

In Creative and Marketing Fields

- Artist
- Playwright
- Novelist
- Poet
- Sales copywriter
- Marketing consultant (expert)
- Philosopher
- Interior designer
- Informational-graphics designer
- Universal design architect
- Freelance media planner
- Editor/art director (magazine)
- Genealogist
- Multimedia producer
- Editor/art director (websites)
- Film editor
- Documentary filmmaker
- Set designer

- Educational software developer
- Exhibit designer
- Costume and wardrobe specialist
- Merchandise designer and displayer

Corporate and Technology

- Staff advocate
- Project manager
- Human resources recruiter
- Human resources manager
- Marketer of ideas and/or services
- Job analyst
- Corporate/team trainer
- Merchandise planner
- Environmental lawyer
- Planned-giving officer
- Philanthropic consultant
- Curator
- Literary agent
- Outplacement consultant

Education, Counseling, Health Care and Social Service

- Social scientist
- Mental health counselor
- Dietitian/nutritionist
- Speech language pathologist/ audiologist
- Holistic health practitioner
- Occupational therapist
- Chiropractor
- Grant coordinator
- Fund-raising director
- Legal mediator
- Adult daycare coordinator
- Corrective therapist
- Legislative assistant
- Director, social service agency
- Massage therapist

GOING DEEPER EXERCISE

After reading through the list of careers, answer the following questions.

Which 5-10 careers jump out at you as something you'd enjoy doing?

_____

_____

_____

_____

_____

Thinking back to the sections on strengths, what do you notice about the list of careers? What strengths might contribute to success in these careers?

_____

_____

_____

_____

_____

Is your current career or career path on the list? If it isn't, how does it stack up against the list of workplace criteria? Could it still be an environment in which you find success?

_____

_____

_____

_____

_____

THRIVING AT WORK

There is an astronomical difference between a job you're good at and a career you love and in which you thrive.

While some people are fine just getting by, people like you and I sure aren't. This section will help you thrive at work.

Three Foundations for Thriving at Work

1) Be aware of your strengths and weaknesses and be selective of the work you do. Be honest in job interviews about where you excel as well as where you struggle.

2) When in a job, take this same honest approach with your supervisor. Explain that you aren't being lazy; rather you feel you could deliver much more *value* to the company by focusing on your strengths.

3) At least once per week, if not daily, stop for a few minutes and ask yourself: "Am I working in my strengths or struggling in my weaknesses?"

4) Remember, you have unique and valuable gifts. Make the effort to use them and avoid getting trapped in the wrong kind of work.

Secret Weapons At Work

When it comes to your work, be sure to tap into these work related strengths for INFJs:

- An ability to understand and empathize with others.

63

- An internal drive to achieve goals and be productive. INFJs like making things happen.

- A sense of loyalty and a deep commitment to succeed at work they believe in.

- INFJs have the potential to be excellent mentors and bosses. Their patience, understanding, and high expectations of others make them excellent "people developers." They see the potential in others and work hard to help them grow.

  Author's note: I have an INFJ mentor myself and have witnessed this first hand.

- INFJs can be logical and rational in how they work yet are also creative. This makes them excellent scientist types who have the ability to "think beyond" current discoveries and come up with new ideas or approaches.

- INFJs are intelligent and have no problem focusing. This gives them an ability to grasp difficult ideas and work on one thing until completion.

- INFJs commit to finishing what they start. If they take on a project or goal, they will focus and work on it until they reach their desired outcome. INFJs aren't afraid of hard work and their persistence inspires colleagues.

- INFJs are interested in systems and determining the best ways to get things done. Couple this with their strong drive to succeed and you can understand why INFJs are very good at achieving their goals.

- INFJs have an ability to see the big picture and use this knowledge to predict the consequences of certain actions or ideas.

- The ability to commit and make 'final' decisions (decisiveness).

- INFJs can develop excellent organizational skills.

KRYPTONITE AT WORK

To maximize their success, INFJs should be aware of some challenges they face at work. INFJs will not always, but *may:*

- Be impatient with people or organizations they see as uncooperative or ineffective. This can play out as the employee feeling smarter than their boss and angry that their contributions aren't properly rewarded.

- Have difficulty working on projects that conflict with their values. Some people are able to sell ice to Eskimos, or fake stocks to senior citizens. Fortunately, INFJs are not. Morally this is good, but practically it can cause problems for INFJs who finds themselves working for Enron or BP.

- Avoid conflict and confrontation, leave problems unresolved, or ignore unpleasantness or problems that should be addressed. This can lead to increased tension and hostility within the workplace.

- Stemming from their avoidance of confrontation, INFJs may be reluctant to confront and discipline those they manage.

- INFJs may shy away from competitive work environments because of the inherent tension and conflict they produce. This can be a shame, since INFJs are very high performers.

- Be stubborn or stuck in their ways. Once they flex their "decisive" muscle and make a decision, INFJs are reluctant to step backwards and revisit it. Similarly, an INFJ's ability to focus and commit can manifest itself negatively as inflexibility.

- INFJs may struggle to simplify and explain complex ideas in a reasonable timeframe.

- Have trouble changing plans or direction when the situation calls for it. In this way, the INFJ is not as adaptable as their other Idealist counterparts, the ENFPs, INFPs, and ENFJs.

GOING DEEPER EXERCISE

Have any of the strengths or weaknesses listed in this chapter been brought to your attention by a boss or colleague before?

_____

_____

_____

_____

_____

Which of the strengths did you instantly recognize in yourself? Are they any you've been underutilizing in your current career?

_____

_____

_____

_____

_____

Which one or two weaknesses, if you were to totally overcome them, would have the greatest positive impact on your career?

_____

_____

_____

_____

_____

RICH AND HAPPY RELATIONSHIPS

Whoever said opposites attract never met an ENFP + ISTJ couple.

Sure, you want a partner who complements your strengths and weaknesses, but most of us also want someone who understands us - someone with whom we can express our opinions and ideas and be understood.

In this section, we'll start with a discussion on what INFJs are like in relationships. Then we'll look at the most common personality types INFJs are happy with. Lastly, we will end with some advice on creating and maintaining successful relationships as an INFJ, and *with* an INFJ.

INFJs In Relationships

INFJs seek intense and powerful relationships full of romance and meaning. They demand a lot from their relationships but are willing to give a lot at the same time. Within their romantic relationships, INFJs are warm and loving partners.

INFJs tend to buy into the idea of fairy tale romance and the existence of a perfect relationship. On a positive note, this belief encourages them to work hard at creating a great relationship. On a negative note, some INFJs may be too quick to jump ship when challenges arise. This stems from the fairy tale ideal and the idea that "if we are perfect for each other then we wouldn't have any problems or challenges."

INFJs are loyal and desire a long-term, committed relationship. When they feel they have found the right person, they are ready and willing to invest themselves in creating the perfect relationship.

INFJs' Ideal Matches

A note on compatibility: There is no be all and end all. The information on type compatibility is based on either theory or surveys, neither of which will ever provide a universal rule.

According to surveys, NF (idealist) types find the greatest relationship *satisfaction* dating other NFs. For an INFJ this means dating ENFPs, INFPs, ENFJs, and other INFJs. This is likely because Idealists share a common way of thinking and feeling about the world.

According to relationship theory, INFJ's two most compatible matches for partnership in building a life (or business) are ENTPs and ENFPs.

Don't take these suggestions as limits to who you can be with. Ultimately, the two individuals, and their desire to grow and work to create an incredible relationship, will be the biggest determination of their success together.

With that said, one incompatibility I've noticed time and time again is between Intuitives (N) and Sensors (S). I think this is because these two groups have fundamentally different ways of interacting with the world and often have trouble understanding one another.

In my own experience in romantic relationships, friendships, and business partnerships, I (a strong Intuitive - ENFP), have always run into trouble with strong Sensors.

Beyond that caveat, it's all up in the air. Generally, for organization sake, I would suggest that P's match with a J. The P will benefit from the J's structure and organization, and the J will benefit from the P's creativity and spontaneity.

TIPS FOR DATING AS AN INFJ

- INFJs have a strong dislike of conflict, criticism, and confrontation. As an INFJ, you will benefit from developing your ability to handle conflict. The only way to do this is with baby steps, one awkward conversation at a time.

- INFJs are excellent partners and loyal companions. Value yourself and what you bring to the table. Take time to access those you date and determine if they can match your standards of loyalty or affection.

- You may set very high expectations for yourself and your partner. Just remember: Everyone is human, and no partner or relationship will be perfect. Don't be too hard on your partner or yourself.

- If you're after a "perfect" relationship, take time to check in with your partner on this. Does he or she share your same high expectations and willingness to work at the relationship? If so, is their vision of a "perfect" relationship the same as yours? Communication around your goals and desires is essential to avoid conflict and disappointment.

- You may have trouble hitting the eject button on a bad relationship. If your relationship isn't meeting your needs, speak to someone you trust for an objective opinion. Your loyalty, caring, and desire to make things work could be blinding you to reality.

TIPS FOR DATING AN INFJ

- INFJs are affectionate, warm, and loving partners. They are also honest and loyal. If they commit to a relationship, they mean it.
  Be clear about your own intentions and desires as they relate to your relationship. Don't string an INFJ along if you aren't serious. If you are all in, make sure they know and feel the same way. I speak to this more in the last point.

- INFJs are highly intuitive and will see through most lies, b.s., and false fronts. Be honest and authentic or you'll lose their respect.

- INFJs may have trouble expressing their feelings. Try and help them along by providing opportunities to casually discuss feelings or situations without judgment. Show them you care and that you're genuinely interested in their happiness.

- Some INFJs struggle with organization, personal finances, and keeping a schedule. If you want to build a life with an INFJ, you must accept this and accept them. Develop systems, hire help, or take responsibility for the details of your life together.

- INFJs have good communication skills but they also have a strong dislike of conflict, criticism, and confrontation. As the partner, you need to be aware of this and may need to initiate difficult conversations and encourage the INFJ to open up and share how they really feel.

  One way to help people open up is to approach the conversation in a friendly and loving way, and to be clear that you will accept and love them no matter what they communicate.

- Because they throw themselves fully into relationships, INFJs can be wary of showing their cards or putting their heart on the line too early. They will look for signs that you're not serious or may leave town as a way to protect themselves from heartbreak. If you're serious about the relationship, make sure they know it.

To learn more about how all the types relate and interact, download the free compatibility chart at:

www.PersonalityTypesTraining.com/Thrive

KEYS TO WEALTH, HEALTH, HAPPINESS, AND SUCCESS

I hope this book has provided some insights into how you can succeed in the most important areas of your life.

In this section, I'd like to share ten strategies for finding all around success. These strategies will help you enjoy more wealth, health, and happiness in your life.

1. INFJs must follow their passions and do work aligned with their values and beliefs.

    Work hard to integrate your introverted intuition with your extroverted feeling function. In other words, take time to understand and think about new people and ideas before passing judgment.

2. Learn to express your feelings even though it is uncomfortable for you, or could cause discomfort to someone else.

3. Value your own feelings and needs as much as you value those of other people.

4. INFJs can sometimes be too hard on other people and have unrealistic expectations for what relationships should be like. Fuelled by Disney movies and Usher songs, INFJs can be quick to skip town the moment their partner reveals a flaw or when a challenge presents itself in the relationship.

5. INFJs will be well served to sit back and *objectively* look at themselves. You may discover you're not perfect either (and that's OK). It can help to enroll a friend or former partner in this process.

6. INFJs have a distain for confrontation, conflict, and being told what to do. In the real world, there will be times when you need to follow orders or engage in confrontation.

    When this happens and negative emotions come up, take a moment to understand and process them. You may think to yourself: "I'm feeling upset and I think it is because I am being told what to do."

    Then, allow your intuition to think it through before you take the mature and productive action that you need to.

7. Face your fears to overcome your weaknesses. Learn to express your opinions in the face of criticism. Learn to be decisive. Learn to be comfortable with confrontation. You will only learn by doing. This means taking action and risking failure. At first this may be very uncomfortable but over time you will develop your abilities and taking action will get easier and easier.

8. Learn to understand others. You have a unique and wonderful way of looking at the world... but it is your own perspective and may not always be right for other people. Learn to understand how other people see the world and your influence will increase while the amount of conflict in your world decreases.

9. Be accountable and take personal responsibility. It is important to be aware of your weaknesses, but do not use this knowledge as an excuse. Never blame others. When you blame others for your circumstances, you give away the power to change them. Take responsibility for your life and you give yourself the power to change it.

10. Take care of yourself. When it comes to health, INFJs will benefit from stress-relieving activities. Consider yoga, meditation, or martial arts as ways to clear your mind

and lower your stress (and blood pressure). In terms of mental health, consider engaging the services of a lifestyle coach or therapist.

PRACTICAL SOLUTIONS TO COMMON CHALLENGES

There is an old-fashioned attitude that tells us to just tough it up, overcome our weaknesses, and do everything ourselves.

This is stupid.

If you're an exceptional painter you should spend your time painting and leave the toilet cleaning to someone else. If you struggle with negotiation, there is nothing wrong with asking a friend or partner to come along and offer support.

The more you allow yourself to offload the tasks and situations you don't enjoy, the more success you will experience. For an INFJ, certain experiences can cause a lot of unnecessary stress and, honestly, there is often just no reason to experience this stress.

With that said, all Idealists will benefit from learning to face their problems and handle confrontation. The suggestions below are meant to ease the pain and help in the learning process, rather than be solutions to increase avoidance. Whereas INFJs should just offload day-to-day chores to a maid or assistant, they will benefit from (gradually) facing their emotional weaknesses and building some tolerance for confrontation and difficult situations. They key here is to improve in baby steps. Strive to take on smaller conflicts yourself while (at least for now) seeking help for more intense situations.

Here are a few practical ideas for making the most of your strengths while avoiding your weaknesses.

Get Help or Support with:

- Accounting
- Cleaning
- Laundry
- Planning Travel
- Organization
- Scheduling
- Life Planning (such as a coach)
- Business Planning

Handling conflict or taking on overwhelming situations. An example would be offloading business disputes to a capable lawyer so you can focus on creation and growing your business.

IMPROVING YOUR SOCIAL SKILLS

When I published the first version of this book, I had many readers contact me and ask for more advice around social situations. The following sections are simply a response to this request and not an assertion that INFJs need this advice or haven't already figured it out.

So, if you already consider yourself a social butterfly, feel free to skip this section.

Social Skills Training and Advice on Social Situations

In our always-on, always-connected society of e-mail, text messaging, and, well, anything but face-to-face conversation, social situations can be a challenge for everyone. We merely do not have as many opportunities to practice conversation as we used to.

As Introverts, INFJs enjoy time alone and are around others even less than their Extrovert counterparts. This means even less time for the natural practice and development of social skills.

Does this mean Introverts are doomed to a life of awkward interactions and social anxiety? Absolutely not. In fact, it is quite the contrary.

When they invest time into developing their social skills, Introverts can become just as capable in social situations as Extroverts. This gives them a well-rounded personality and an excellent advantage: the ability to chat and socialize when they want, and to sit quietly and listen to others when the situation calls for it. No one likes the person who always has to be the center of attention, right?

This chapter is broken into seven sections, each covering a particular social skill or social situation. At the end of the chapter, you will find a list of additional resources if you would like to continue working on your social skills.

BEING INTERESTED

I have heard it said that being interested in others is the fastest route to becoming the most interesting person in the room. Show a genuine interest in others and you will unquestionably be well liked.

When you take an interest in another person, a few powerful things happen.

1. You build rapport and the other person starts to like you.
2. You learn important details about the other person. You can then use these details to create conversation around common interests.

When learning about another person, what you ask is almost as important as how you ask it. Typical small talk questions like "So what do you do?" are as boring as they are uninformative. Try using some of the questions below and you will find yourself in much more stimulating conversations.

- What is your biggest goal for this year?
  (Can be followed up by: Why? What challenges do you see coming up?)
- What is your favorite part about your career/hobby/relationship/hometown?
- What is the biggest challenge you are currently facing in your work/school/life?
- I have noticed that you are really good at (insert something you have noticed – for example their style, conversation, telling jokes, business, or cooking). What is your secret? Could you share 2 or 3 tips for an amateur like me?

When you are asking questions about their goals or challenges, you are giving yourself an opportunity to offer advice or help them find a solution. You will be amazed at how far this can go, and how much more stimulating the conversation can become when you are working on solving a problem.

In terms of how you approach this, just be curious and thoughtful in your mindset and you will do just fine.

GETTING OUTSIDE OF YOURSELF

The curious thing is, most people at social events are all thinking the same thing: "I wonder what other people are thinking about me."

When you come to realize and truly accept this, everything changes. If you are friendly and kind, you will be amazed at how many people will be drawn to you (especially other Introverts!).

Of course, much of our anxiety in social situations goes back to the same thought playing in our heads: "I wonder what others are thinking about me."

How do you get past this? Look no further than the last tip: Be genuinely interested in other people. When you move your focus to understanding and caring about others, it is almost impossible to focus on yourself at the same time.

SAY SOMETHING PLEASANT

One compliment can, and will, change someone's whole night.

So why don't we give people more compliments? One reason is that we get stuck in our heads, wondering what to say and how to say it. We worry about coming off as inauthentic, offending someone, or appearing like a kiss ass. We wonder whether our compliment could be misinterpreted, or get us into an awkward situation. Although all these fears are normal, they are also all unfounded.

The key to giving an excellent compliment is in the details, so pay attention to them. Some people spend hours picking out their outfits - nothing is left to chance. Sometimes there will be an obvious "point of pride," such as a new dress or piece of jewelry the person is just waiting to be complimented on. Other times it might not be so obvious, so try these tips:

- For a man, his watch or tie is always a safe compliment (from a man or a woman). From a woman to a man, well, you can get away with complimenting anything.
- For women, jewelry, purses, and shoes are always a point of pride and a safe compliment from another woman.

For the guys, it is a little more complicated. If you don't know the woman well, keep it casual in what you compliment and how you say it. Fashionable jewelry, a trendy phone case or a colorful watch are safe bets and good conversation starters. Follow up your compliment by asking where they got it or if there is a groovy story behind it. For example, "That's a really cool watch. Is there a story behind it?"

If you already know the woman, a new hairstyle or piece of clothing is also begging for your compliment.

- Always be as authentic as possible. Look for something you do like in someone, whether it is something physical or a character trait. You will never upset someone by mentioning their excellent sense of humor.
- Sometimes you will be able to notice an area someone is trying to improve, and perhaps is self-conscious about. For instance, you may notice a fellow Introvert making a

big effort to be social and is telling a story to a group of people. This is an amazing opportunity.... Use it.

It's not hard to say, "That was really funny. You know, you are a wonderful storyteller." A few kind words on your part here could make an unforgettable impact and go a long way in building their confidence and encouraging them to continue growing. In doing so, not only do you make someone else feel great, you also make them feel good about you.

PLEASE AND THANK YOU

One of the challenges many introvert types face is a dislike of doing things "just because," particularly when it comes to social norms and etiquette. To the outside world, it can appear as rude or inconsiderate when an INFJ does not say thank you to their host for having them over for dinner. In reality, the INFJ may be very appreciative, they just don't see the need for pleasantries (or they just forgot). They may also take it for granted, assuming the other person knows how much they care about them, or they are assuming a close friend does not need to be thanked.

The problem is, some people are overly sensitive or just stuck in their ways. Sometimes a lack of "etiquette" can cause unnecessary hostility or conflict, especially with those who do not know you as well, such as a good friend's spouse.

Two things you can do:

Option 1: Make an effort to build habits around manners and etiquette. Perhaps it does not make sense to thank someone for passing the salt, but just do it anyway.

Option 2: Take a few minutes to speak to, or write a note to the most important people in your life. Tell them how much you value your relationship and explain to them that social norms are not exactly your thing. Make it clear how much you value them and everything they do for you, even if you do not express it at the moment they do something for you.

Once a year, say around Christmas, send out handwritten cards to your closest friends and make sure to include a note about how much you appreciate them and how happy you are that they are part of your life.

If you do these two things, not only will they not care when you forget a "thank you," you will stand out as one of the most caring and thoughtful people they know.

EXPLAINING NERVES AND SOCIAL ANXIETY

As we walked into one of our regular cafés, my girlfriend reminded me to say hi to her friend working there. "She was upset you did not say goodbye last time."

This sparked a conversation on "Hi and Bye" etiquette, and approaching people working or in a group. I explained that most of the time when someone does not come over and say hi they are not trying to be rude. Usually there is something else going on. Often this something else is nervousness, or social anxiety. Approaching a group of people to say hello when you only know one or two of them can cause much stress. Logically it probably should not, but alas, it does. One option is to face the nerves and awkwardly approach the group, and then stand there waiting to be invited to sit or for the right time to walk away. The other option is a brief wave, or to pretend you did not see them, and move on. In this case, you risk being considered rude, or having people think you do not like them, or think you are mad at them.

Isn't it funny, the wide gap between two people's perceptions?

Unfortunately, there is no magic cure for this situation although, for the sake of personal growth, I would encourage you to try to say hello whenever possible.

There is, however, a way you can limit the potential damage (and possibly make the situation a lot easier in the future).

The solution is along the same lines as the one in the "Please and Thank You" section. You need to initiate an honest discussion with friends. For an extreme Introvert, the idea of being nervous about approaching a group of people is almost confusing. To them, the only possible explanation is rudeness or a disinterest in them.

Yet guess what happens when you explain the situation from your point of view? They start to understand. Not only will they "get it" when you do not approach them within a group, they may even spot you first and come over to you to say hello.

Note: In this section, I use the term social anxiety to describe nervousness or anxiety around situations. If the negative emotions are so strong that they negatively influence your life, or the anxiety is constant, we may be talking about a more serious form of social anxiety. If this sounds like you, I encourage you to read:

Self Confidence Secrets: How To Overcome Anxiety, Fear, and Low Self Esteem With NLP.

I have received many e-mails from readers telling me that this book has helped them overcome (sometimes crippling) social anxiety and build their confidence.

AVOID CRITICIZING AND COMPLAINING

You are at a social event and you feel uncomfortable. You didn't really want to go in the first place, and now you are dreading your decision to "give it a try." You find yourself at the bar when a fellow guest, equally disappointed, strikes up a conversation:

"Why are these things always so boring? This might be the worst one yet."

Now it is your turn to speak. How do you respond?

It is easy to fall into this negativity trap. Being critical of others is one of the easiest ways to feel better about yourself (in the moment) and temporarily bond with others. The problem is that it's a short-term solution with many negative long-term consequences. Complaining and criticizing brings you down emotionally, eliminates any drive to become more social, and almost guarantees the night will not get any better.

What's more is that when you become a complainer you repel the people you would have the most fun talking with, and the ones who are likely in charge of deciding who will be invited back.

Sure, in that moment, never being invited back may sound like a blessing. But would it not be better to be invited back and just decline the invitation if you do not want to go?

ESCAPING THE SMALL TALK TRAP: DIRECT THE CONVERSATION, ASK QUESTIONS, AND GET HELP

Nothing is worse than the *Small Talk Trap*. You are at a social event where you hardly know anyone and find yourself in a conversation with a stranger. Initially the conversation provides relief from the awkward agony of "working the room," but soon the conversation is just as painful. You find yourself thinking back to biology class, wondering how much long-term damage would come from jumping out the second story window behind you and making a run for it.

It doesn't have to be like this! There is a better way.

Here are three skills you can use to make your conversations more stimulating.

Strategy #1 - Direct It. There is a good chance that the other person does not want to talk about the weather any more than you do. But even if they do, why leave it up to them?

When you go to an event, have a few thought-provoking topics in mind. Ideally, these should be interesting to you and to the kind of people you like to talk to. An example could be a book you just read about another culture or a philosophy you have been studying. When the weather comes up in conversation for the third time, then it is definitely time to change the subject with this simple phrase:

"Hey, sorry to interrupt, but I would love your opinion on something before I forget. I have been reading this book on Stoic philosophy and it has been bombarding me with ideas about how to live life. I keep wondering how these ideas can relate to our modern lifestyle. Do you know much about Stoicism?"

At this point, if they are familiar with the topic, that's great. If they are not, this becomes a chance for you to explain the subject to them. In doing so, you will crystalize your knowledge of the topic and hopefully teach them something interesting in the process.

Sure, some will not have a lot to say, but others will. Either way, you will have a much better time in this conversation than in one about weather or sports!

Strategy #2 - Ask Questions. Most people have at least one worthwhile trait or area of knowledge. If you find yourself trapped in a painful conversation, use it as your chance to learn something new.

Start by asking a few quick background questions about the person's home country, work, or hobbies. From there you will be able to find something thought-provoking to zero in on and learn more about. Are they from a far-off country you have always wanted to know more about? Turn this into an opportunity to learn a few phrases in a new language, to discover a few cultural differences, or ask about possible economic opportunities. Perhaps they study a martial art you have always wanted to learn. You could ask them for advice on the best way to get started, and then how to spend your first three months in your new venture.

It won't always be the most fascinating conversation, but it's still better than typical small talk.

Strategy #3 - Get Help. This one can be trickier, but once mastered, is a ninja skill of social situations. If you are speaking one-on-one with someone and the conversation is leaving a lot to be desired, try to bring another person in.

The easiest way to do this is when you spot someone you know, or a stranger standing alone, just motion for them to join you. If this is not an option, there is always Plan B. Take the conversation to a point where you need an opinion on something. Perhaps you decide to disagree on what city has the best weather, or which appetizer at the party is best. Whatever it is, use it as an opportunity to seek another opinion from someone walking or standing nearby: "Excuse me, we were just debating this and would love another opinion. What do you think ...?"

However you do it, two things can happen when you bring in a new person.

One, they could be a stimulating conversationalist and change your night for the better. Often when this happens, your original conversation partner will eventually excuse themselves and you will be left with an enjoyable conversation and possibly a new friend. If the conversation does not improve, at least you have given yourself a less awkward escape route because you will not be leaving anyone alone.

Another upside of this approach is that you may be saving someone else from the awkwardness of standing alone and they will be grateful for it.

ADDITIONAL RESOURCES ON SOCIAL SKILLS

If you enjoyed this section and want to continue your study of people and social skills, here are a few books to get you started.

All the titles below are linked to the book's page on Amazon so you can read more about it.

Networking for People Who Hate Networking: A Field Guide for Introverts, the Overwhelmed, and the Underconnected

Self-Promotion for Introverts: The Quiet Guide to Getting Ahead

The Introverted Leader: Building on Your Quiet Strength

Quiet: The Power of Introverts in a World That Can't Stop Talking

Quiet Influence: The Introvert's Guide to Making a Difference

The Introvert Advantage: Making the Most of Your Inner Strengths

QUOTES TO MAKE AN INFJ SMILE

To end, I've included a collection of fun, inspiring, and relatable quotes for INFJs. Many are from INFJs, others are simply enjoyable for INFJs.

"I feel all shadows of the universe multiplied deep inside my skin."

-Virginia Wolfe

"I don't consider myself a pessimist at all. I think of a pessimist as someone who is waiting for it to rain. And I [am already] completely soaked to the skin."

Leonard Cohen

"To live is to suffer, to survive is to find some meaning in the suffering."

-Nietzsche

"I often feel like I want to think something but I can't find the language that coincides with the thoughts, so it remains felt, not thought. Sometimes I feel like I'm thinking in Swedish without knowing Swedish."

-Anna Kamienska

"And the fact that it bothers me bothers me also."

-Nietzsche

"You," he said, "are a terribly real thing in a terribly false world, and that, I believe, is why you are in so much pain."

-Nietzsche

"It is a great art: to love and keep still."

-Anna Kamienska

"I don't understand why Alice left Wonderland."

-E.M. Forster

"People who know my heart never have to question it."

-Anna Kamienska

"I am just striving to be more me than I have ever been."

-Anna Kamienska

"Let yourself go. Pull out from the depths those thoughts that you do not understand, and spread them out in the sunlight and know the meaning of them."

-E.M. Forster

"And that's the thing about people who mean everything they say. They think everyone else does too."

-K. Hosseini

"Live intentionally, feel everything, love achingly, give impeccably. Let go."

-E.M. Forster

"You don't want to say the wrong thing. I've seen [people] hurt for years over something that was unnecessary and didn't have to be said."

Al Pacino

"The little girl just could not sleep because her thoughts were way too deep, her mind had gone out for a stroll and fallen down the rabbit hole."

-E.M. Forster

"You have the answer. Just get quiet enough to hear it."

-Pat Obuchowski

"Few are those who see with their own eyes and feel with their own hearts."

-Albert Einstein

"Night is purer than day; it is better for thinking and loving and dreaming. At night everything is more intense, more true. The echo of words that have been spoken during the day take on a new and deeper meaning."

-Elie Wiesel

"When all else fades, my soul will dance with you, where the love lasts forever."

-Elie Wiesel

"Live the full life of the mind, exhilarated by new ideas, intoxicated by the romance of the unusual."

-Ernest Hemingway

"Your flaws are perfect for the heart that is meant to love you."

-K. Hosseini

"Be bold and be brave and trust in your heart. It knows things you cannot imagine. Trust that it understands better than you can ever realize. It can never be Bravery if you never feel scared."

-Tyler Knott Gregson

"Thrive in the truth."

-Ernest Hemingway

"I feel there is nothing more truly artistic than to love people."

-Vincent Van Gogh

"The work you do when you procrastinate is probably the work you should be doing for the rest of your life."

-Jessica Hische

"Maybe one day we will find a place where our dreams and reality collide."

-Jessica Hische

"Let yourself be drawn by the strange pull of what you love, it will not lead you astray."

-Rumi

"If you cannot explain it simply, you do not understand it enough."

-Albert Einstein

"There is a voice inside of you that whispers all day long 'I feel that this is right for me, I know that this is wrong.' No teacher, preacher, parent, friend, or wise man can decide what's right for you - just listen to the voice that speaks inside."

-Shel Silverstein

"A bird sitting on a tree is never afraid of the branch breaking, because its trust is not on the branch but on its own wings."

-Shel Silverstein

"Promise me you will not spend so much time treading water and trying to keep your head above the waves that you forget, truly forget, how much you have always loved to swim."

-Tyler Knott Gregson

"The worst thing is watching someone drown and not being able to convince them that they can save themselves by just standing up."

-Shel Silverstein

"I am indeed a practical dreamer. ...I want to convert my dreams into realities as far as possible."

-Mahatma Gandhi

"Power consists in one's capacity to link his will with the purpose of others, to lead by reason and a gift of cooperation."

-Woodrow Wilson

"Doubt kills more dreams than failure ever will."

-Shel Silverstein

SUGGESTIONS AND FEEDBACK

Like the field of psychology, this book will always be growing and improving.

If there is something about this book you didn't like, or there is a point you disagreed with, I'd love to hear from you. Perhaps I missed something in my research.

As well, if you are an "experienced" INFJ and you'd like to add your personal story, insight, wisdom, or advice to upcoming editions, my readers and I would love to hear from you.

To contribute in any way, you can email me at: dan@dreamsaroundtheworld.com

A SMALL FAVOR

If you enjoyed this book or found it useful, I'd be very grateful if you'd post a short review on Amazon. Your support really does make a difference, and I read all the reviews personally. So I can get your feedback and make this book even better.

If you'd like to leave a review, then all you need to do is visit this book's page on Amazon.

Thanks again for your support!

NEXT STEPS

To help you get the most from this book, I have created a collection of free extras to support you along the way. If you haven't done so already, take a few minutes now to request the free bonuses; you already paid for them when you bought this book. To download these, simply visit the special section of my website. There, you will be asked to enter your email address so that I can send you the "Thriving Bonus Pack." You'll receive:

-A 5-part mini-course, delivered via email, packed with tips on adjusting your life to maximize your strengths.

-A compatibility chart showing how you are most likely to relate to the other 15 personality types. You'll discover which types you're most compatible with and which will likely lead to headaches.

-A PDF workbook designed to complement this book. It's formatted to be printed, so you can fill in your answers to the exercises in each chapter as you go.

To download the Thriving Bonus Pack, visit:

www.PersonalityTypesTraining.com/Thrive

Books In The Thrive Personality Type Series

The ENFP Superhero : Harness your gifts, Inspire others and Thrive as an ENFP

Or just visit Amazon and search for "ENFP". Then look for the book by Dan Johnston.

INFP Inspired: Embrace your true self and thrive as an INFP

Or just visit Amazon and search for "INFP". Then look for the book by Dan Johnston.

ENFJ on fire: Utilize your gifts, Change the world and thrive as an ENFJ

Or just visit Amazon and search for "ENFJ". Then look for the book by Dan Johnston.

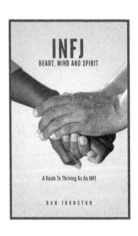

INFJ, Heart, Mind and Spirit: A Guide to thriving as an INFJ

Or just visit Amazon and search for "INFJ". Then look for the book by Dan Johnston.

The Well Rounded ENTJ: Find more harmony, Improve relationships and thrive as a natural leader

Or just visit Amazon and search for "ENTJ". Then look for the book by Dan Johnston.

INTJ Understood: Harness your strengths and thrive as the unstoppable mastermind

Or just visit Amazon and search for "INTJ". Then look for the book by Dan Johnston.

The ENTP Plan: Invent yourself, make progress and thrive as the charming and visionary ENTP

Or just visit Amazon and search for "ENTP". Then look for the book by Dan Johnston.

INTP: Utilize your strengths, solve life's problems and thrive as the genius thinker type INTP

Or just visit Amazon and search for "INTP". Then look for the book by Dan Johnston.

Thrive Series Collections

The Idealists: Learning To Thrive As, and With, ENFPs, INFPs, ENFJs and INFJs (A Collection Of Four Books From The Thrive Series)

The Rationals: Learning To Thrive As, and With, The INTJ, ENTJ, INTP and ENTP Personality Types (A Collection of Four Books From The Thrive Series)

About The Author

Dan Johnston is a #1 international best-selling author, speaker, coach, and recognized expert in the fields of confidence, psychology and personal transformation. As a coach, one of his specialties is helping clients discover their natural talents, apply them to their true purpose and create a plan of action to live the life of their dreams.

Dan publishes new videos weekly on his YouTube Channel. Here you will hundreds of videos on psychology and personality type.

This is the best place to catch Dan's latest content: www.YouTube.com/DreamsAroundTheWorld/

If you prefer to listen, check our Dan's podcast here: www.DreamsAroundTheWorld.com/podcast

To learn more about Dan Johnston and his coaching services visit:
www.DreamsAroundTheWorld.com/coaching

For articles, interviews and resources on entrepreneurship, pursuing your passions, travel and creating the life of your dreams, visit Dreams Around The World and subscribe to the "The Life Design Approach":

www.DreamsAroundTheWorld.com

**Find more books By Dan Johnston on his Amazon Author
Central Pages:**
Amazon.com:
http://www.amazon.com/author/danjohnston

Amazon.co.uk:
http://www.amazon.co.uk/-/e/B00E1DO6OS

Never Settle – A Short Article

This is an article I wrote for revolution. It is on a topic near and dear to my heart. I've included it in this book to let you learn a little bit more about me, and hopefully to inspire you to think big and always go after your dreams. Dan.

Never Settle

"That is seriously your life? You are literally living the dream. That's insane."

I've grown to expect this every time I tell someone about my fairy-tale of a life. But trust me, it wasn't always this way.

A lot people put off travel, passions and happiness until some distant future point; be it the sale of their business, a promotion, or retirement. I used to be one of them.

I owned my own business and I worked like a dog with the dream of one day "making it". Then I could make happiness a priority. I sacrificed friendships, health, family and travel opportunities all because I had to work harder for "just a little while longer." I just needed to "make it" and then things would be different. Then I could I finally start enjoying life.

That was until my business imploded and left me completely, and I mean completely, broke. To get it started I needed to co-sign all the business loans and other liabilities, and so when the business failed so did I. Rock bottom occurred. Public failure. Massive financial stress. All that sort of good stuff.

I can actually remember one night when I was terrified my date would show up hungry because so much as grabbing a pizza together would mean I couldn't afford pasta and milk the following week. I now refer to this time of my life as my "Pursuit of Happyness" phase.

But life must go on, right? What was I going to do, marry a government employee, move to Idaho and get a job as an accountant? Not in this lifetime. And for the record, what the hell does "making it" even mean?!

Fast-forward about 10 months and I'm working as a freelancer and still struggling. It's Saturday evening and the weather is just miserable. Dark clouds, drizzling rain, cold enough to be uncomfortable yet not like a romantic Christmas cold you get bundled up for and almost enjoy. I was at home thinking about my situation and suddenly was overcome with emotions. Where was the light at the end of the tunnel? Something has to change or I'm not going to make it.

I knew I needed to make a serious change in my life because I couldn't handle the stress much longer. The clear decision was to "Call It Quits" and move back home for a bit. Start applying for jobs, save up a little money, and start rebuilding my life.

Lucky for me the windows were fogged that night and I wasn't seeing clearly. Fuelled by half a bottle of red wine and a desire to live true to myself and my word, I booked a one-way ticket to Costa Rica.

Two weeks later, with less than a month's living expenses in the bank and no steady income I was off to the airport and I had no idea what awaited me on the other side.

It was a huge risk...and it paid off.

The change of scener reset my emotional clock. The sun beamed energy into my heart and soul. My business grew, like really grew. Four weeks after arriving in Costa Rica, I called my little brother and surprised him with a plane ticket to come visit me the following week. And yes, I could now afford to treat my date to a pepperoni pizza.

This was early 2012. Since then I've lived in 5 countries, heading towards my 6th next week (Barcelona, Spain). I've crossed countless items from my bucket list including driving a Lamborghini on my birthday, speaking Spanish, playing with a baby monkey, learning to surf and driving a Hank Moody inspired Porsche up Highway 101.

When things got hard I had plenty of opportunities to raise the white flag. To retreat. To turn my back on the life I really wanted.

I'm sure you'll have the same opportunities. Ignore them.

Don't ever, ever think going for it, going after what you really want, will be easy.

But it will always, always be worth it.

For More Visit:

www.DreamsAroundTheWorld.com

Exclusive Reader-Only Bonuses:

To help you get the most from this book I have created a collection of free extras to support you along the way.

When you visit the site below you will be able to download a printable workbook to record your reflections and answers to the end of chapter exercises.

You will also receive free enrollment in a Five-Part E-Course on personality psychology delivered by e-mail. The training is packed with tips, strategies, advice and additional resources.

Through the five lessons, you will learn how to implement what you have learnt about your personality type, including:

- How To Learn From Your Mistakes and Gain Experience Fast
- Why You Must, and How You Can, Become The Best In The World
- How to Overcome Your Weak Spots
- How to Put Your Strengths into Action and Achieve Your Highest Potential.
- How To Pay It Forward By Understanding Those Around You and Helping Them Become Their Best Selves

Both are yours free, a special thank you for my readers.

To receive your free companion course and workbook, visit:

www.dreamsaroundtheworld.com/thrive

Made in the USA
Columbia, SC
19 September 2020